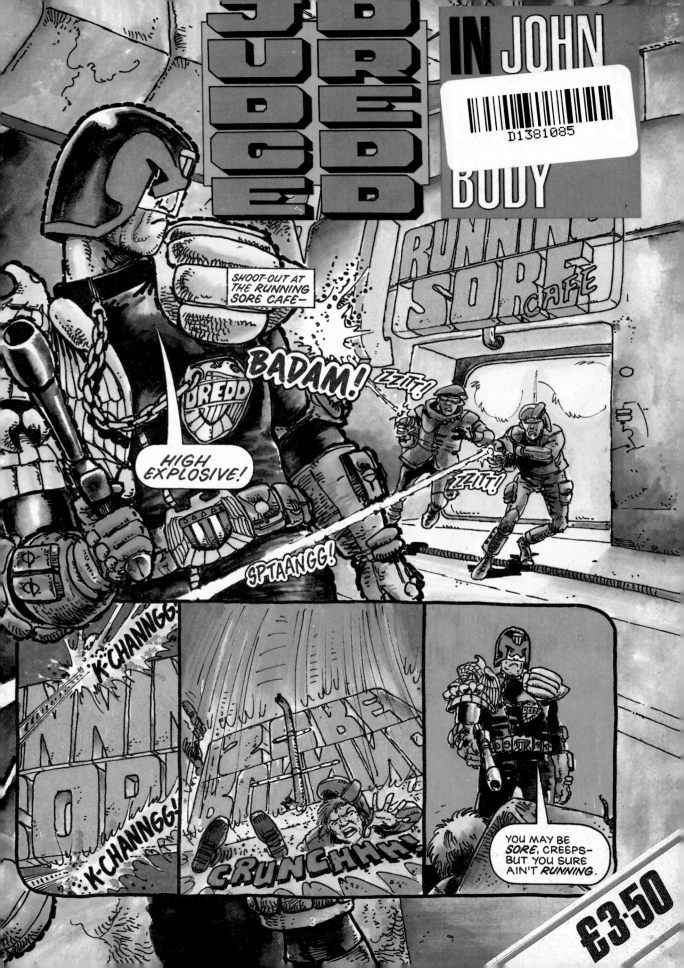

YOU GET THE ONE *YOU* WERE AFTER, *ROOKIE?*

VRRRMMMM!

YES, SIR! HE LED ME QUITE A CHASE, BUT I CAUGHT HIM!

NAME OF *JOHN BROWN*, TWO PREVIOUS *AR!Vs*, VARIOUS MINOR CONVICTIONS.

SO WHERE IS HE?

LEFT HIM CUFFED TO A RAILING ON HAYTE STREET.

HAYTE STREET? ARE YOU *CRAZY?*

B-BUT HE'S NOT GOING ANYWHERE—

DON'T BE SO SURE! *WITH ME!*

WELL WELL, WHAT HAVE WE GOT HERE?

HAYTE STREET

L-LISTEN, YOU JUVES, GET ME LOOSE AND I'LL GIVE YOU A *THOUSAND CREDS!*

YOU DON'T *GIVE* US NOTHIN', TURKEY!

WHAT WE WANT, WE *TAKE!*

SLICE!

RRRIP!

GET OFF!

4

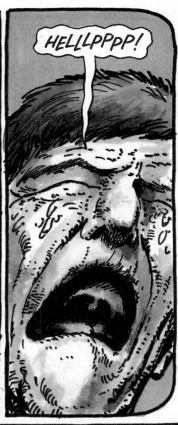

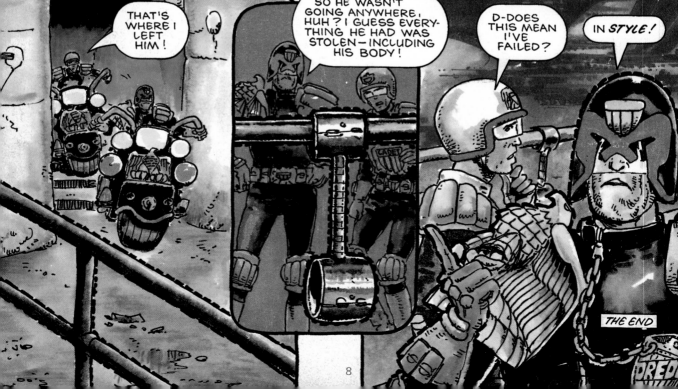

THE END

8

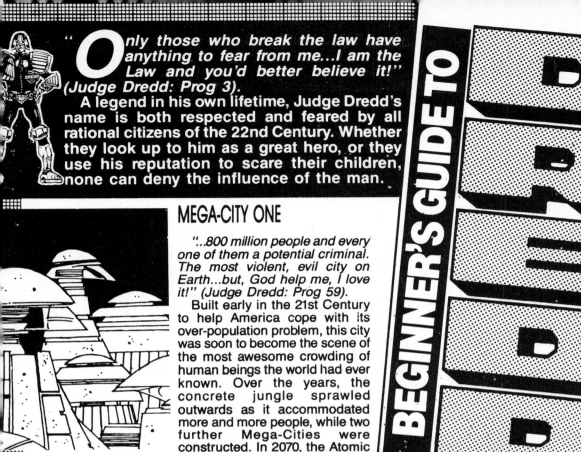

"*Only those who break the law have anything to fear from me...I am the Law and you'd better believe it!*" (Judge Dredd: Prog 3).

A legend in his own lifetime, Judge Dredd's name is both respected and feared by all rational citizens of the 22nd Century. Whether they look up to him as a great hero, or they use his reputation to scare their children, none can deny the influence of the man.

BEGINNER'S GUIDE TO DREDD

MEGA-CITY ONE

"*...800 million people and every one of them a potential criminal. The most violent, evil city on Earth...but, God help me, I love it!*" (Judge Dredd: Prog 59).

Built early in the 21st Century to help America cope with its over-population problem, this city was soon to become the scene of the most awesome crowding of human beings the world had ever known. Over the years, the concrete jungle sprawled outwards as it accommodated more and more people, while two further Mega-Cities were constructed. In 2070, the Atomic Wars saw most of America destroyed, but Mega-City One escaped large scale damage, resulting in a new influx of people. By 2099, the population of the city had reached 800 million. However, the Apocalypse War of 2104, a second nuclear conflict, resulted in the annihilation of half the city and its inhabitants. Still the place remains incredibly huge and complex, with well over 1000 million miles of roadway in constant use!

THE JUDGES

"*It takes fifteen years to train a Judge. Fifteen years in the toughest school on Earth. Fifteen years of iron discipline...rigid self-control...concentrated aggression! By the time a Judge hits the streets he is no longer a man...he is a machine!*" (narrative: Prog 178).

With Mega-Cities a new concept in human habitation, a new system of policing them to maintain law and order was required. Therefore, the United States' government established the Judges, who would be highly

trained, incorruptible upholders of justice, invested with extensive powers of arrest and on-the-spot sentencing. They would be led by a Chief Judge. Judge Fargo was the first to be appointed to this post in Mega-City One, giving him a large say in the running of the city. However, the position of the Judges in society meant that they had to be proved worthy of the trust placed in them, so their training and testing had to be extremely rigorous. For the purpose of training cadets, the Academy of Law was built, with the intake of pupils coming only from children under five and infant clones, bred by the Justice Department itself. After admission, they would then spend fifteen very hard years training in all aspects of law enforcement, under constant threat of expulsion for the smallest failing. Only a small percentage of candidates graduate as full Judges, but the ones who do are the only people who stand a chance of lasting five minutes on the deadly streets of Mega-City One! When President Robert L. Booth initiated the Atomic Wars of 2070, the angry citizens demanded his removal from office and petitioned the Judges to take over the government. Thus, Chief Judge Clarence Goodman, top man at the Justice Dept., became the ultimate ruler of Mega-City One from then on, until his death in 2100, to be followed by all subsequent Chief Judges.

JUDGE JOE DREDD

"A Judge should have no deep-rooted fears...no terrors that haunt him. Fifteen years training should see to that. Of course, some Judges are only human... others aren't!" (narrative: Prog 190).

The toughest and most resourceful of all the Judges, Dredd is a very authoritative figure and supremely confident in his own abilities. Extremely strong of both will and limb, he fearlessly carries out his duties, often fighting on against incredible odds. He derives much of his talent from having been cloned, along with his brother Rico, from the DNA structure of Judge Fargo, first Chief Judge of Mega-City One. Throughout his

training at the Academy of Law, Joe was known for his thoroughly straight character and quickly earned the nickname, "Old Stoney Face", even though his brother was always a little better at most things than him. Despite having only been born in 2066, they were both able to graduate in 2079 with honours, but almost at once, Rico took up petty crime. He even found time to father a daughter, Vienna, before Joe was forced to make the hardest arrest of his life — that of his brother! Thus the career of the most distinguished Judge of all time began with a personal tragedy. But Dredd was trained from the start not to betray any sentiment about such things. As years passed, his reputation grew and he quickly assumed status as a senior Judge.

HIS GREATEST MISSION
The Robot Wars (Progs 10-17).

"We give robots the will to live and then expect them to die like willing slaves. It's going to spell trouble one day! How long will it be before robots discover how to break the law?" (Judge Dredd: Prog 9).

A fault in the obedience circuit in the carpenter robot, "Call-me-Kenneth", caused the machine to go berserk on a killing rampage through the city. Fortunately, Dredd soon disabled and captured it, but then it was rebuilt in an improved form and escaped once more, before the fault could be corrected. On that occasion it appealed to all robots in a dramatic TV appearance and thus inspired a full-scale robot rebellion. A devastating war between the Judges and the robots followed, with Kenneth building more robots, all pre-programmed to hate humans, and to provide reinforcements for his army. However, Dredd eventually managed to subvert the production process with the aid of Walter the Robot and a few other pro-human robots and, after an enormous amount of bloodshed, the revolt was put down. Unfortunately, "Call-me-Kenneth" remained at large to rampage once more through Mega-City One, causing further death and destruction. Dredd, who had sworn to deal with the

rogue android, quickly caught up with him. Acting fast, one well-aimed shot from Dredd saw the robot utterly destroyed in a massive explosion! The robot wars were finally over, with millions dead.

The Cursed Earth (Progs 61-85).

"When someone calls on the Law for help...be he mutie, alien, cyborg or human...the Law cannot turn a blind eye! And I am the Law!" (Judge Dredd: Prog 69).

Tweak

An horrific disease had broken out in Mega-City Two, causing people to turn into mad cannibals. In Mega-City One, they had developed an antidote, but plague victims had taken over the Mega-City Two Spaceport, making it impossible for them to fly in the cure. Therefore, a mission had to be mounted to carry the vaccine across the nuclear wastes of the Cursed Earth, between the two cities. Dredd was requested to lead a squad of hand picked men. On their journey, they had to deal with all manner of threats: mutants, dinosaurs, slavers, outcasts, war-droids and various other radiation-spawned hazards. Despite the seriousness of his main mission, Dredd still involved himself in any situation where he could bring justice. At great personal risk, he rescued Tweak, an intelligent alien, from a gang of slavers. The trek continued, but the Cursed Earth took a terrible toll on the lives of the travellers. Finally, as they reached their goal, only Dredd and Tweak survived, but between them they carried enough of the vaccine to save the city from an agonising death.

The Day the Law Died (Progs 89-108).

"There are going to be some changes around here, and the sooner that you and the people all learn that, the better. I am Chief Judge now...I am the Law!" (Chief Judge Cal: Prog 89).

Having secretly ordered the murder of Chief Judge Goodman, Deputy Chief Cal took over his post and began a reign of terror as dictator of Mega-City One. When Dredd discovered Cal was involved in the killing, Cal had to order his assassination. Shot through the head, Dredd barely survived the attack, but aided by Judge Giant, he was able to evade Cal's forces and begin planning resistance to the corrupt Chief Judge.

As Judge Cal had managed to submit most of the Judges to a type of brainwashing, to make them subservient to him, recruiting Judges to his cause proved difficult for Dredd, and he found his main help came from old, retired Judges from the Academy of law. Even so, the oppressive nature of Cal's rule soon saw mass demonstrations on the streets by the citizens, greatly inspired by Dredd's small resistance group. Unfortunately as they were on the verge of a successful insurrection, Cal called on the Kleggs, a vicious race of alien mercenaries, who, with sudden shock of their arrival, were able to beat the citizens and Dredd's band into a hasty retreat.

With his regime thus bolstered, the resistance fight became a long and protracted struggle, while Cal's new laws became even more repressive. To stop the citizens escaping into the Cursed Earth, he ordered the construction of a vast wall around the city and, during this period, he twice sentenced the whole city to death — as well as outlawing happiness! Finally, the rebels were forced to act quickly when Cal looked set to make good his threat to release nerve gas over Mega-City One. By subverting the Chief Judge's brainwashing of the Judges, the "rebels" were able to gain many new allies, and with this new strength they were able to kill Cal just in time to save the city and restore sanity to the Judges' leadership, with the appointment of Judge Griffin as the new Chief Judge.

The Quest for the Judge Child (Progs 156-181).

"Somewhere out there is the child that can save my city. I'll find him...or I'll never return to Mega-City One!" (Judge Dredd: Prog 161).

Dying Judge Feyy, made a final prediction of disaster for Mega-City One in 2120, unless the "Judge Child", Owen Krysler, could be found and made Chief Judge by that time. Dredd was entrusted with the mission to find the boy. Picking up his trail, Dredd headed out into the Cursed Earth and finally on to Texas City. But before Dredd could catch up with Owen, the boy was captured by a family of cut-throat criminals, the Angel Gang, who promptly escaped with their prize into space. Returning to Mega-City One, Dredd led a small squad of Judges on board the Justice 1 Spacecraft on a quest across the galaxy for the "Judge Child". During their mission, their search for clues as to the whereabouts of the Angel Gang saw the death of one crew member as they had to deal with many types of alien civilisations and colonies.

Eventually, they reached the planet Xanadu, where the Angels made their last stand. But Link and Mean Angel soon met their deaths at the hands of Judge Dredd. Pa and Junior Angel retreated rapidly into "Grunwald's Kingdom", a robot free-state, but Dredd was undaunted and pursued them. Finally, he killed the two remaining Angels and rescued Owen Krysler, while the Grunwalder, mysterious ruler of the state, stood by and wisely made no attempt to obstruct Dredd in his mission. Having found the "Judge Child", Dredd decided to leave him with the Grunwalder instead of taking him back to Mega-City One, since during his quest to find the boy, Dredd had found evidence to show that the boy was touched by a streak of evil, making him utterly unsuitable to become a future Chief Judge of Mega-City One!

Judge Cal

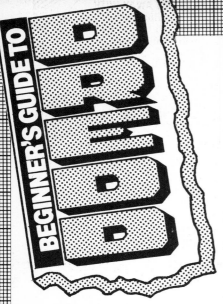

The Apocalypse War (Progs 245-270).

"Only yesterday I was pulling in perps on these streets. Now there aren't any perps. There aren't even any streets." (Judge Domer: Prog 251).

By lacing Mega-City One's water supply with a drug which induced citizens to turn to violence, East-Meg One spy Orlok was able to cause a massive outbreak of Block Wars throughout the city. With the Judges busy trying to deal with this disaster, East-Meg One launched a nuclear assault on its North American counterpart. Virtually automatically, Mega-City One made its counter-strike, but the Sovs were greatly protected from the missiles, by their newly

developed Apocalypse Warp, which warped the oncoming nuclear warheads into another dimension. Having destroyed roughly half of Mega-City One, the Sovs launched their more conventional forces under the command of War-Marshal Kazan. The American Judges fought bravely, but their cause seemed hopeless, especially when Chief Judge Griffin was captured and brainwashed into betraying them. Natural leader of the resistance, Dredd was forced to kill Griffin before the Sovs could use him for excessive propaganda, that threatened to kill off the morale of the Mega-City citizens.

Desperate for a way to fight back, Dredd formed the "Apocalypse Squad", a hand-picked, elite group of Judges with one mission...to win the war! Judges Anderson, Hershey, Ocks, Kwan, Costa, McDonald, Hamble and Morant made up the eight Judges that Dredd used in his last-ditch attempt to take the war back to the Sovs. Capturing a Sov Strato-V flying craft, they sped towards East-Meg One and, with the element of surprise, they managed to take over a Sov missile silo. From there they launched an attack on East-Meg One which led to the utter annihilation of the city! With their homeland destroyed, the Sov invaders in Mega-City One soon lost their will to fight and the Judges regained control of their own city under the new leadership of Chief Judge McGruder. Nevertheless, it was a

long time before Mega-City One recovered from this holocaust.

City of the Damned (Progs 393-406).

"The Chief Judge must be pure...above corruption. We know that from past experience. The boy was evil. He could only bring disaster upon us! Whatever danger is to come, we must face it on our own. If we perish...so be it." (Judge Dredd: Prog 181).

By 2107, five years after Judge Feyy's prediction of disaster for Mega-City One in 2120, scientists had successfully developed a functioning time machine. Chief Judge McGruder decided to send Judges Dredd and Anderson forward 13 years in the prototype time machine, Proteus, to check out what will actually happen. On arriving in 2120, they discovered the city in ruins and the Judges degenerated into vampires, that literally fed off the blood of the citizens. This had been brought about by a creature that called itself "The Mutant" — a being with incredible mind powers. In time, the two Judges discovered the Mutant was, in fact, a hideously deformed clone of the "Judge Child", Owen Krysler, who was out for revenge. The Mutant was delighted with the opportunity to take revenge on Dredd himself again, having already killed the Dredd of 2120 and turned him into a mindless zombie. So, having first blinded Dredd and pitted all kinds of monsters against him, the Mutant set the zombie Dredd on to him in a duel to the death! It was obviously a battle Dredd could not win, being up against an already dead version of himself. He and Anderson took flight. Realising that if he could get back to 2107, the Mutant could be beaten, Dredd tried to reach Proteus and, despite being constantly pursued by the zombie, the two Judges made it and successfully reached their own time. Armed now with the knowledge that it is the Grunwalder who will attempt to clone the "Judge Child", thus producing the super-powerful Mutant by accident, the Judges decided that he must be destroyed as a complete safeguard!

Apocalypse War

JUDGE DREDD
'A FISTFUL OF DENIMITE'

PSI-DIVISION TELEPATH **JUDGE ANDERSON** ARRIVES AT THE SCENE OF A CRIME —

THIEF GOT AWAY WITH TWELVE THOUSAND CREDS FROM THE OFFICE BOX. WATCHMAN MUST'VE DISTURBED HIM — TOOK A BULLET FOR HIS TROUBLE!

NIGHTWATCHMAN? THOUGHT THEY WENT OUT WITH THE ARK.

YOU FIGURE THE COST OF A ROBOT — UPKEEP — CITY TAX — SOMETIMES IT WORKS OUT CHEAPER TO HIRE A HUMAN. ESPECIALLY FOR THE PEANUTS THESE SUCKERS WORK FOR.

WELL, THIS SUCKER'S BEEN DEAD TOO LONG FOR ME TO READ ANY **LATENTS.**

WE GOT A SCRAP OF CLOTHING OFF THE FENCE BARBS.

BLUE DENIMITE — PERP'S SHIRT, MOST LIKELY. FORENSIC'S WAITING, BUT I HELD ON TO IT IN CASE **YOU** COULD PICK UP SOMETHING.

BLOOD ON IT. GOOD! MIGHT MAKE IT EASIER...

THAT SMALL SCRAP OF DENIMITE IS THE BRIDGE — THE **LINK** BETWEEN ANDERSON'S EXTRAORDINARY MIND —

— AND THE MIND OF A COLD-BLOODED KILLER!

I SEE A MAN... RUNNING... HE'S HURT...!

AHEAD OF HIM — BRIGHT LIGHTS, PEOPLE... NOISE. IT'S AN AMUSEMENT PARK. HE'S GOING IN. HE FEELS... SAFE THERE.

THERE'S **FUNTAZIA** DOWN ON THE HEYNESWAY.

OKAY. I'LL PICK HIM UP!

FUNTAZIA! RIGHT. LET'S SEE HOW SAFE YOU ARE, CREEP!

THE PSI-JUDGE LETS HER EXTRA-SENSORY POWER GUIDE HER INTO THE HEART OF THE FUNFAIR —

CREEP'S CLOSE — I CAN SENSE IT!

14

SHE SENSES THE BLOW EVEN AS IT DESCENDS —

RUN FOR IT, STIV!

I'LL FIX — UUNNGH!

YOU'RE DOIN' TIME TOO, CREEP!

ANDERSON GIVES CHASE —

CAN'T RISK A SHOT. TOO MANY PEOPLE!

HE'S JUMPED ONTO THE FLIPPERZIPPER!

GO FOR IT!

HEY, STIV! WHAT'S THE MATTER —
I GOT BAD BREATH OR
SOMETHIN'?

KEEP BACK! KEEP BACK OR
THE BRAT GETS IT!

TUT TUT, STIV! YOU DISAPPOINT ME.
THERE'S NO NEED FOR VIOLENCE —

AT LEAST,
NOT FROM **YOU**,
MEATBALL!

HE'S
GOING
OVER!

RUNNING
OUT ON ME
AGAIN,
STIV?

READERS' Art SPECIAL

Draw th

THE DEATH OF DREDD?
Drawn by Richard Freemantle, Breaston, Derby.

JUDGE DEATH

IN THE NECK OF THE LAW
By Lex Andrew, Barrhead, Glasgow.

THE YOUNG ONE
By Declan Kennan, Armargh, N. Ireland.

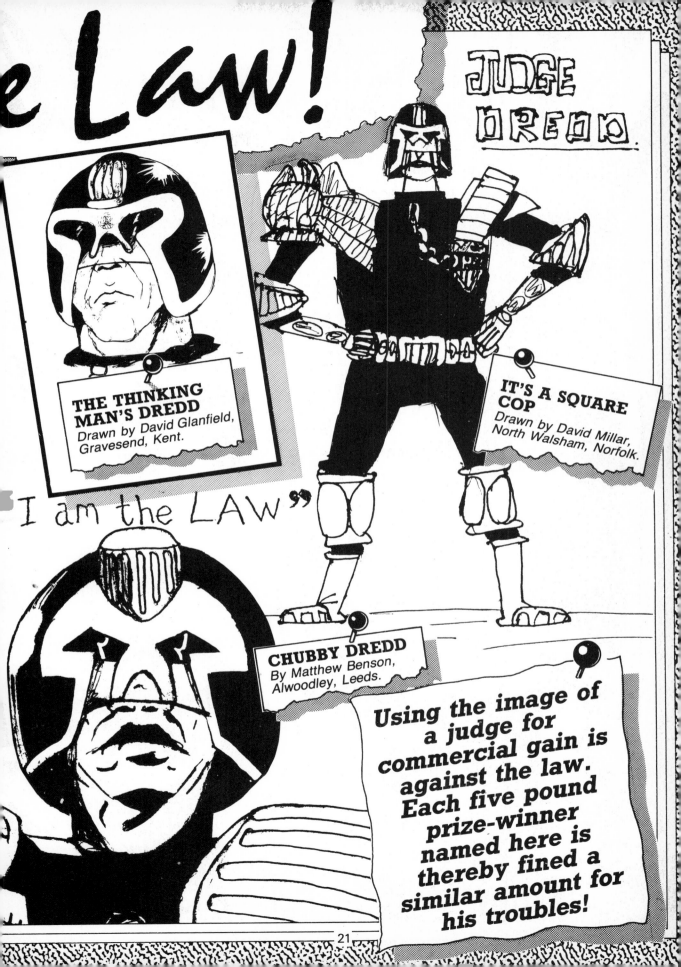

e Law!

JUDGE DREDD

THE THINKING MAN'S DREDD
Drawn by David Glanfield, Gravesend, Kent.

IT'S A SQUARE COP
Drawn by David Millar, North Walsham, Norfolk.

"I am the LAW"

CHUBBY DREDD
By Matthew Benson, Alwoodley, Leeds.

Using the image of a judge for commercial gain is against the law. Each five pound prize-winner named here is thereby fined a similar amount for his troubles!

The Rookie

WHUMPPAA!

"You got him, Jacko! You got a judge!"

Dekker watched the three juveniles run blindly through the smoke created by their home-made explosive device. She glanced at the judge beside her and flipped her belt communicator to transmit. The juves could wait.

"This is Dekker. Judge Cara needs a med-team, urgent, corner of IPA Plaza and 101." She looked down at Cara's neck, at the point where her finger was lightly pressed against the vein. "Scratch the medics. Make that a meat wagon."

Up now and running, Lawgiver held tightly in her hand, Dekker assessed the situation: 'Three males... already used one clumsy high-ex, might have a second with them...*judge-killers!*'

As she turned the corner, she saw the flash of a gun and dived into a roll, raising and firing her weapon in one smooth movement. The juve hit the ground, clutching his belly, crying out to his friends that he was hurt. One down; two to go.

The others made a run for it. The hunched youth called Jacko trying to prime another bomb, the taller youth attempting to aim his weapon at Dekker as he sprinted for cover. Dekker's bullet took him through the neck, spinning his body over the dusty slidewalk.

Her next shot nicked Jacko's wrist, the pain contorting his face, the impact sending his domestic high-ex spiralling to the ground. Jacko stared in horror as it smashed against the concrete. It didn't go off. Then he felt the warm barrel of a Lawgiver pressing hard against his temple.

"Lousy craftsmanship. You're under arrest. Move."

Sector House 29 wasn't the place to be if you were looking for peace and quiet. The corridors were crammed with suspects being brought in for interrogation, and perps being taken out for the haul to the iso-cubes. Even

Dekker had already considered, and rejected, the possibility that she was to blame for Cara's death. She didn't even think *Cara* was to blame for Cara's death. He simply died on duty, taking the risks a judge was trained to take every day. She thought the Captain would see it that way, too.

"Captain Gurvitz wants you in his office now, Dekker."

Gurvitz didn't want to reprimand her, he wanted her to take on the highest responsibility that can be given to a judge.

"You want me to assess a rookie judge on street patrol?"

"That's right, Dekker. Strictly speaking, you're not senior enough for such a duty — but I've been impressed with your performance to date, and I think the city can benefit from your experience. I want you to decide if this rookie's fit to wear the full eagle."

The judiciary system of Mega-City One revolved around the training of cadets to become qualified judges — rigorous training over fifteen hard years. Ultimately, though, only observation of a rookie under street combat conditions would tell if he was fit to wear the black helmet and full eagle of a true judge.

"If you think this rookie fails to make the grade, Dekker, it is your solemn duty to fail him. However, I want you to bear something in mind..."

Gurvitz fixed his eyes on the traffic mayhem that took place on the other side of his office window every hour of every day. "The city has already spent several million credits training this rookie — credits that will be thrown into the gutter if he doesn't come up to expectations. I'm asking you to accept a heavy responsibility. You must not waste municipal funds — but on no account must you allow a bad apple to enter our ranks."

MEN ONLY!

The rookie was waiting in the corridor outside. The file in Gurvitz's office had given Dekker all the essential data...his height, weight, temperature; his ability with a Lawgiver, his control of the 2500cc turbo-cycle christened 'The Lawmaster'...there was more, but Dekker knew it was down to her to discover the critical information.

"Mitchell? I'm Dekker. Let's go!"

She tried to guess if he was nervous. It wouldn't mean much if he was — she remembered how nervous she'd been as a rookie under Judge Dredd. "You were a rookie under Dredd, weren't you?" he asked. She wondered if he could read minds, in which case he belonged over in Psi Division. "That's right."

Mitchell grinned at her: "I heard he passed you as the best rookie he'd ever assessed. That's some testimonial!" Dekker led the way down the steps to the Bike Compound, moving directly to the pair of gleaming Lawmasters standing side by side. The rookie spoke again as they straddled their machines:

if Dekker had wanted to reflect on the meaning of life, Robens, the clerk from Captain Gurvitz's office, wouldn't have let her.

"The Captain will see you in two minutes, Dekker. Guess you're pretty nervous, huh?"

"Should I be?"

Robens smiled: "Sure! Judge Cara puts in four years service on the streets, then he goes out on patrol with you and whammo! — just 24 hours later he's a stiff!" Dekker cleared her throat. "Can I be frank with you, Robens? You're a creep!"

The Rookie

"Imagine...assessed by the greatest judge who ever lived! It's like getting a vote of confidence from a legend!"

Dekker gunned her engine into life, and Mitchell followed suit. "Let me ask you a question, Mitchell. Who said: 'There is no room in the life of a judge for elevation of the personality'?" Dekker started to crawl up the exit ramp, Mitchell pulling himself up alongside her. He didn't know the answer. "It was Dredd — the legend himself. So let's drop the hero-worship. Okay?"

Radio Control brought the exchange to an abrupt end: "Multiple homicide. Panzer Plaza!"

The Lawmaster went up a gear, leaning into the wind as they accelerated out of the Sector House and on to the teeming skedway. "Responding!" Dekker and her rookie were going to work!

The Plaza looked like the scene of a wild party. Med-team transports and meat wagons were everywhere, their flashing blue and red lights trying to compete with each other. A large crowd had gathered to watch the fun, to stare at the latest victims of the blood-lust that was everyday life in Mega-City One. One of the medics had all the necessary data: "Six stiffs, judge, plus one survivor — in a bad way."

"Did he say anything?"

"Yeah...said he was walking past some husband and wife team having an argument. Seems the wife pulled out a gun and took a shot at her old man. She didn't kill him, though, so he grabbed it off her and let rip." Dekker looked at the body-bags on the ground and put two and two together. First, the creep kills his wife; then he has a go at a few passers-by, just for the hell of it. Another crazy citizen in a city full of crazies.

"You reckon the wife had the first shot...did she get him?" Mitchell called her over from the other end of the Plaza. "I've found a trail of blood," said the rookie. "It heads off into the Consumer Services Precinct." Dekker took out her Lawgiver. "She got him. Let's move!"

You don't need 15 years of training to follow a trail of blood-spits to a closed door. Mitchell looked at the sign above his head and glanced at Dekker. "Uh...you take the back, I'll go through and flush him out. Right?" Dekker followed his eyes back to the neon sign: UNCLE SAMMY'S SAUNA — STRICTLY MEN ONLY. "Wrong. I'm a judge, Mitchell — I go wherever the law takes me." Dekker strode into the hot, steamy room, brushing aside the stunned attendant, pointing her Lawgiver at the broiling male citizenry inside.

"Freeze."

More than a dozen men stared back at her in horror — all dripping with sweat, all desperately groping for towels as they realised a woman was staring straight at them. Another time, Dekker might have found the sight amusing; but not now. "Hands above heads." Her voice rang through the silent chamber, but no-one moved. Then, a squeak from the back: "It's a lady judge! I mean, h-holy cremol..."

"DO IT!" The towels hit the floor simultaneously, as every hand in the room reached for the ceiling...every hand except one, which came out from under a towel holding a blaster, and started to squeeze on the trigger. But Mitchell's hand was faster!

The crazy killer slid down the wall, the blood from his chest mingling with his own sweat and the steam of the sauna. Nobody moved to pick up their towels.

Back out on the Plaza, Radio Control was informed of the body count. "You made a mistake back there, rookie." Dekker's tone was hard and unrelenting. "If you ever pull that...that *chivalry* stuff again, you can wave goodbye to your eagle." Mitchell climbed on his Lawmaster. It hadn't been a serious error of judgement, but enough to give a word of warning. "Is that understood?"

" I guess I thought of you as a woman not a judge. Stupid. It won't happen again."

"Good." Dekker swung her leg over her own machine. "It had better not!"

COLD CORPSE

Over the following weeks, Dekker had the chance to observe her rookie under normal street conditions — normal by the lunatic standards of Mega-City One, that is. In accordance with the Judicial Training Procedure Manual, she kept a log, recording Mitchell's performance for later review...

"ITEM: Elderly citizen caught in possession of 3 kilos illegal white sugar. Claimed he had a sweet plasti-denture. Rookie waived mandatory 5-year-stretch, suggested psycho cube observation. Correct decision under circumstances."

"ITEM: Passed group of revellers in costume. Mitchell saw one wearing mock-up of judge's uniform. Gave him 6 months hard. Punishment straight out of textbook, of course — but approve rookie's explanation to perp's mother as to why such impersonations are strictly forbidden. Showed good moral tone."

"ITEM: Excellent control of his Lawmaster to apprehend juves speeding on skedway. When one of juves opened fire, he displayed good balance to keep up speed and return fire. Managed to hit their vehicle, sending it crashing through shopette window, impact fatal. Rookie explained compensation procedure to owner of shopette with textbook mixture of sympathy and firmness."

"ITEM: Mitchell obliged to scatter dangerously large crowd. More authority is needed in his voice projection."

Dekker paused at the computer console and smiled. She remembered when she was a rookie, and Dredd had said the same thing to her about vocal expressions of authority. She went back to the keyboard...

"ITEM: Believe Mitchell needs one more street operation before I can be certain he is fit for full eagle — some form of criminal activity more serious, more demanding than those he's had to cope with to date."

And then the killings started!

The call summoned them to Lord Byron Block. The caretaker was worried: "It's the guy in 361/D — I haven't seen him for nearly two days." Dekker was unimpressed.

"Well, the thing is, judge...I could be wrong, but, uh...I think I heard a shot up there yesterday morning."

"Did you report this?"

"Uh...no. I didn't, y'know, think anything of it at the time." The judges exchanged glances. "Show us the apartment!"

They only tried buzzing 361/D the one time. When they got no answer, they kicked the door off its hinges. The apartment looked clean, with everything in its rightful place, but it was cold — as cold as the corpse in the middle of the room, a hole drilled neatly through the forehead.

Dekker spoke with authority: "I'll call a wagon and take a look around. You deal with that guy."

The caretaker's mouth dropped as Mitchell gripped his arm and started to walk. He was already in the elevator, halfway to the ground floor, when the man finally found his voice.

"Wh-what the heck is goin' on here? What did she mean, 'deal with' me?" The elevator doors slid open. "You failed to report the suspected perpetration of a crime, citizen. That's a serious dereliction of your civic duty — you're going to do time!"

Mitchell dragged his reluctant perp through the block doors, and marched him to the nearest holding-post. He could wait there till the wagon came to take him to the cubes. "Wait a minute, judge! I *did* my duty — it was *me* who called you here today!" "Mitchell to Control. Got a perp to pick up, Lord Byron Block. Six months."

The cuffs were on — no point him struggling anymore. "Yeah, you called us — but you did it too late. If you'd done it yesterday, the killer's trail would still be fresh. Now it'll be harder to find the man who committed the crime." The caretaker stared miserably as the white-helmeted rookie walked back into the block that he used to run.

By the time Mitchell returned to the apartment, Dekker had compiled all the available data on the victim: "Name, P. Kagillian. He was an ex-con, just served a 20-stretch for mob murder. Released ten days ago, along with the three others who'd committed the murder with him."

Mitchell studied the ice blue face of the corpse at his feet. "And now someone's murdered him."

"Full marks for observations. There's more... Central Computer confirms that, since their release, two of those four gang members have been murdered — and P. Kagillian here makes it three out of four. Your assessment, rookie...?"

"It's unlikely to be a coincidence. Perhaps there's a stash of loot hidden away from twenty years back, and the last one alive wants it all for himself." Dekker stared at him. "So he kills the other three?" she asked. "I doubt it. He'd know we'd come looking for him. Got any other ideas?" The rookie knelt down, and looked at the bullet-hole in the ex-con's head, then looked up at the judge in charge of the final stage of his training.

"It could be a revenge killing — someone with a long memory who reckons 20 years in a cube isn't enough of a punishment."

Dekker walked past him and through the shattered remains of the apartment door. "So let's find our fourth man before the killer does."

SHOWDOWN

"Sector Control to Dekker. The man you're looking for is one Howard Rincon. He is not in his apartment. Suggest you investigate warehouse in Old Town, Quadrant 48...he used to run a business from there. Over".

"Drokk it!" Dekker stabbed at the console in front of her. "Computer — give me a new progress chart from current position of Old Town 48!"

Sirens blaring, the Lawmasters changed direction under guidance from their computers — roaring up over the Montana Freeway, cutting across Denver and Lampard, causing even more chaos as they weaved through the snarled-up traffic on Boenders Avenue. Mitchell had to shout above the din. "These revenge killings, they could be an old associate carrying on an ancient grudge, right?"

"Go on," said Dekker.

"Well, it could also be someone closer to the guy these four murdered 20 years ago...it could be family." Dekker nodded. "Computer — I want all the data available on the family of a murder victim back in 2088. Victim's name was Lenny Domm, repeat..." The computer accepted Dekker's input. Then it explained how it would take a while to compile data going that far back into the records. "Great!" said Dekker, "I bet they didn't tell you about

that when you were a cadet!"

Her bike computer was still humming when the Lawmasters slowed to a crawl at the warehouse perimeter in Quad 48. Dekker frowned: "This dump probably hasn't seen electric light since the Apocalypse War. It looks like it's gonna fall down if we breathe too heavily on it!"

"What now, rookie?"

"It sure is bigger than I'd expected...I suggest we split up, Dekker, and circle the building in opposing directions." Mitchell waited for her nod of agreement, then started to ease his bike towards the southerly side of the building. He stopped when he felt Dekker's hand on his arm.

"Remember...we're talking about four hardened perps, all of them killers — and three of them already dead. Get my meaning?" It was Mitchell's turn to nod. "Whoever is responsible for these killings is good at it. We must both exercise extreme caution."

"Let's do that," said Dekker, and turned her bike towards the northerly side of the warehouse.

The battered door was almost the first thing Mitchell saw as he leaned the bike round the corner. He stopped and dismounted, checked that his Lawgiver was primed, and steeled himself for what he might find inside. The ancient timbers creaked as he peered inside the blackened hulk. He could hear the wind rushing along a thousand deserted corridors, he could smell the stench of decay — but he couldn't see a thing.

The rookie crept deeper into the warehouse interior, blinking as he tried to adjust to the darkness. A rat the size of his arm launched himself across his foot and out of sight. He jumped, but he didn't make a sound. Then he saw the corpse...his second one that day.

'Fits Rincon's description', he thought, turning the shiny face into what little light there was. 'The last of the gang of four, murdered like his partners in crime. But he's still warm — we're getting nearer!'

Mitchell's hand reached for his belt radio to summon Dekker to the grisly find. He stopped short of flicking the switch to transmit when his eye caught the movement of a shadow on the wall up ahead. No rat this time, but the reflection of a murderer moving stealthily away from his crime.

Mitchell slowly removed his white helmet; it was catching the light too much. He got to his feet, and inched his way towards the perp. Tiny shards of glass crunched beneath his heavy boots, making less noise, he thought, than the heart thumping wildly inside him; but still the figure cast its shadow on the wall. Now he had reached the corner of the corridor, he could hear his enemy breathing. Mitchell hurled himself around the wall.

"FREEZE!"

His eyes blazed as he stood, feet spread wide apart, Lawgiver pointing rigidly straight ahead. His finger began to squeeze the trigger, but then, suddenly, it relaxed, and he started to lower his hands. The blade sliced into him with sickening ease, forcing its way into his body just below the second rib, penetrating deep inside him. The rookie dropped his Lawgiver, and crumpled to the floor in a heap.

Dekker's computer had finally come up with the goods. "So Lenny Domm left a wife and three sons, huh? They still alive?" she asked. "All four dependants are still alive. Only one member of the family has a criminal record: Tom, the eldest son. Served two years for possession of a replica firearm, six years for malicious behaviour". The computer circuits automatically switched off. Dekker reached for her belt radio: "Mitchell! We could be looking for family after all...could be the victim's eldest boy. Name of Tom Domm, would you believe — aged about 34 by now, previous conviction for violence. Got any thoughts on the subject?" She waited for him to respond. When he didn't she switched to transmit again, this time with more urgency.

"...with previous convictions...*Stomm it!* Mitchell, do you copy?" Mitchell groaned as the hand reached across to remove the crackling receiver from his belt. He knew he was seriously hurt. He found it hard to keep his eyes open, but he had listened to Dekker barking out her message — and now he could hear the sound of his communicator being stamped into pieces beside his helpless body. He groaned again.

Dekker would've guessed by now, she'd have sensed danger. But the knife had been brutally jerked out of his chest, and the rookie judge knew he was losing too much blood, too fast...

The Rookie

The rookie's Lawgiver pointed straight ahead. His finger began to squeeze on the trigger . . . but suddenly he relaxed. Why?

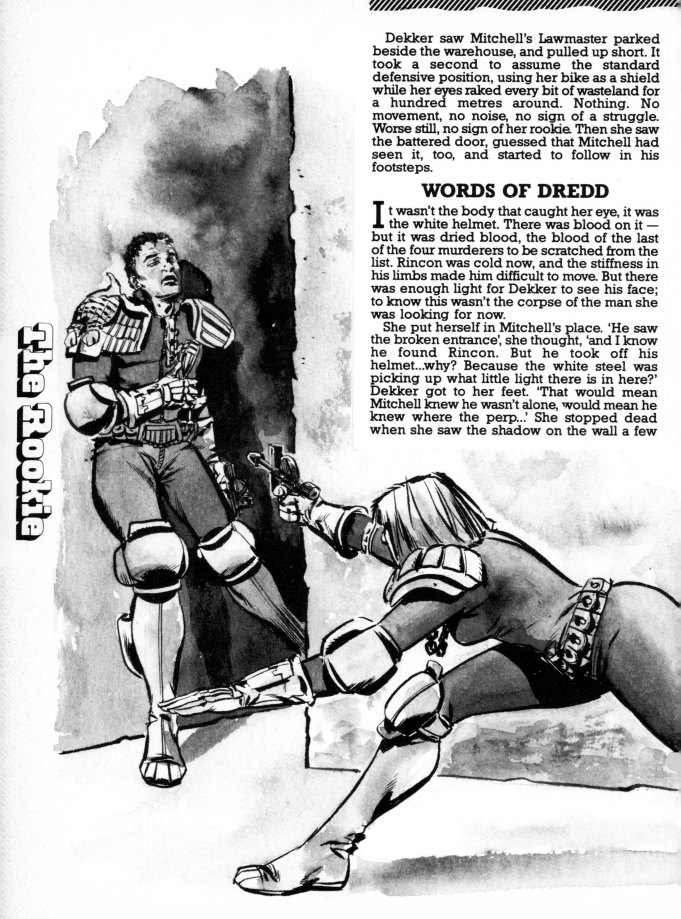

Dekker saw Mitchell's Lawmaster parked beside the warehouse, and pulled up short. It took a second to assume the standard defensive position, using her bike as a shield while her eyes raked every bit of wasteland for a hundred metres around. Nothing. No movement, no noise, no sign of a struggle. Worse still, no sign of her rookie. Then she saw the battered door, guessed that Mitchell had seen it, too, and started to follow in his footsteps.

WORDS OF DREDD

It wasn't the body that caught her eye, it was the white helmet. There was blood on it — but it was dried blood, the blood of the last of the four murderers to be scratched from the list. Rincon was cold now, and the stiffness in his limbs made him difficult to move. But there was enough light for Dekker to see his face; to know this wasn't the corpse of the man she was looking for now.

She put herself in Mitchell's place. 'He saw the broken entrance', she thought, 'and I know he found Rincon. But he took off his helmet...why? Because the white steel was picking up what little light there is in here?' Dekker got to her feet. 'That would mean Mitchell knew he wasn't alone, would mean he knew where the perp...' She stopped dead when she saw the shadow on the wall a few metres further up ahead. Gripping her Lawgiver more firmly, she edged towards it. Her eyes remained fixed on that shadow, watching it sway gently from side to side, as she moved closer...closer...closer...

And then she was moving fast, throwing herself into the corridor, jabbing the barrel of her gun under the face of — Mitchell.

The rookie judge had been propped up against the wall, too weak to resist, too weak to do anything but sway feebly from side to side. His hands clutched at the wound in his chest, trying to stem the flow of his life's blood. Now his eyes were wide open, not looking at Dekker, but staring over her shoulder.

"Mitchell? What the Drokk....?"

Dekker turned just as the knife plunged down at her in an arc of death. Her movement was enough to prevent all but a slash across her arm. She didn't have time to feel it. She was spinning across the dark corridor, slamming her back against the far wall, raising the Lawgiver with her one good arm. She stared into the face of the killer who'd claimed the lives of four hardened ex-cons, perhaps claimed Mitchell, too, and who definitely wanted her to join in the fun.

It was the face of an old woman; sixty, maybe sixty-five. She held the blood-drenched knife up high again, and lunged. Dekker didn't hesitate.

BA-DAMMM!

The high-explosive bullet almost cut the old woman in half. It wasn't necessary to look twice to know that she was dead.

"St-stupid".

Dekker leaned forward and lightly touched Mitchell's face.

"Be quiet. The med-squad is on its way. You're gonna be all right."

Dekker knew the final showdown was near. She threw herself into the corridor and found her gun pointing at a surprising target!

"Chivalry." Mitchell was finding it hard to breathe. He was choking the words out. "S-saw woman. Old woman...h-hesitated. *Grud!* Damned ch-chiv-chiv..."

Judge Dredd shifted uneasily in his seat. He didn't like coming to the Rest and Recreation Room in the Sector House, but he knew it was important to Dekker.

"I take it the old woman was Lenny Domm's widow?" he asked.

"You take it right. Neither of us were expecting her, but I didn't think twice once it happened. Mitchell did — that's why he's dead." Dredd was trying to be patient. "Dekker, a full Commission of Inquiry found you were not culpable of any dereliction of duty leading to the death of that rookie. If you continue to blame yourself, however, your efficiency will be seriously impaired."

"Listen, Joe, I saw his problem long before the warehouse incident. I saw he had this attitude to women, this chivalry — like some kind of knight in shining armour! But I didn't fail him for it...and a different decision would've saved his life."

Dredd shrugged "Maybe. In my judgement, it would have been a misuse of municipal funds to reject a rookie on so slim a basis. That's for one thing — for another, there are plenty of male judges quite capable of making the same fatal hesitation as Mitchell did. And lastly, Dekker, you've learned something from all this."

"I have?" she asked.

"Next time, you'll make sure your rookies realise that everyone in this city — male, female, old, young... everyone is a potential lawbreaker!" Dredd got to his feet. "Thanks for your time, Joe. I appreciate it."

POSTSCRIPT:

The judges had been on patrol for an hour when they spotted the old lady being mugged. When the offenders had been rounded up and cuffed to a holding-post, Scott, the rookie judge, approached the elderly victim.

"You look shaken up. Want me to get Welfare to pay you a visit?"

"Welfare? Naww...I'm fine...no thanks to these bandits!" The words were hardly out of her mouth before she smacked one of her assailants in the face with her sturdy walking stick. Scott slapped the cuffs on her and attached her to the same post as the muggers. "Premeditated assault. Six months."

The rookie glanced across at the judge assigned to the final stage of his training, and walked over to her.

"Uh, Dekker..? You were smiling just now. Did I do something wrong?"

"Not a thing, Scott. You did just fine."

The Lawmaster crackled a new bulletin: "Riot in progress, St. John's Astrodome!"

"Responding!"

Dekker and her new rookie were going to work!

JUDGE DREDD

To honour the men who carry out the law in Mega-City One, the people have erected beside the Statue of Liberty... **THE STATUE OF JUDGEMENT!**

At the top—in the "eye" of the Judge...

Great view! Hey! There's some kinda *disturbance* down below!

Your money, mister—and no jive!

THE DAY THE STATUE WAS UNVEILED...

Wowee! What a statue! From the top they say you can see right across the Mega-City!

FANTASTIC!

But I don't have any money on me... *AAAH!*

33

MEGA-CITY MEDIA QUIZ

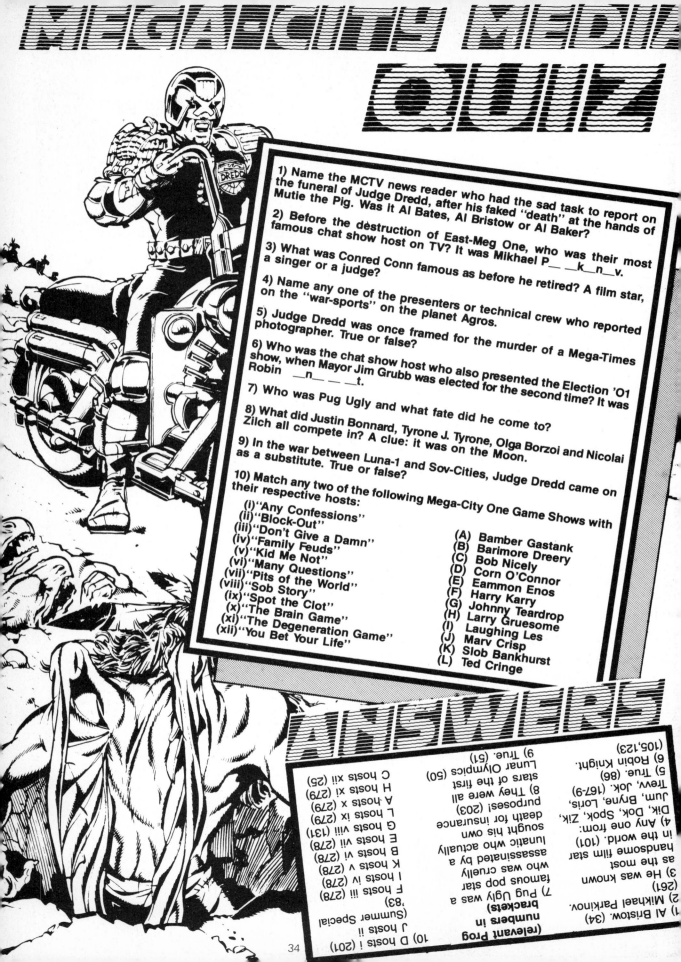

1) Name the MCTV news reader who had the sad task to report on the funeral of Judge Dredd, after his faked "death" at the hands of Mutie the Pig. Was it Al Bates, Al Bristow or Al Baker?

2) Before the destruction of East-Meg One, who was their most famous chat show host on TV? It was Mikhael P__ __k__n__v.

3) What was Conred Conn famous as before he retired? A film star, a singer or a judge?

4) Name any one of the presenters or technical crew who reported on the "war-sports" on the planet Agros.

5) Judge Dredd was once framed for the murder of a Mega-Times photographer. True or false?

6) Who was the chat show host who also presented the Election '01 show, when Mayor Jim Grubb was elected for the second time? It was Robin __n__ __ __t.

7) Who was Pug Ugly and what fate did he come to?

8) What did Justin Bonnard, Tyrone J. Tyrone, Olga Borzoi and Nicolai Zilch all compete in? A clue: it was on the Moon.

9) In the war between Luna-1 and Sov-Cities, Judge Dredd came on as a substitute. True or false?

10) Match any two of the following Mega-City One Game Shows with their respective hosts:

(i) "Any Confessions"
(ii) "Block-Out"
(iii) "Don't Give a Damn"
(iv) "Family Feuds"
(v) "Kid Me Not"
(vi) "Many Questions"
(vii) "Pits of the World"
(viii) "Sob Story"
(ix) "Spot the Clot"
(x) "The Brain Game"
(xi) "The Degeneration Game"
(xii) "You Bet Your Life"

(A) Bamber Gastank
(B) Barimore Dreery
(C) Bob Nicely
(D) Corn O'Connor
(E) Eammon Enos
(F) Harry Karry
(G) Johnny Teardrop
(H) Larry Gruesome
(I) Laughing Les
(J) Marv Crisp
(K) Slob Bankhurst
(L) Ted Cringe

ANSWERS

1) Al Bristow (34)
2) Mikhael Parkinov. (261)
3) He was known as the most handsome film star in the world. (101)
4) Any one from: Dik, Dok, Spok, Zik, Jum, Bryne, Loris, Trevv, Jok. (167-9)
5) True. (86)
6) Robin Knight. (105,123)

(relevant Prog numbers in brackets)

7) Pug Ugly was a famous pop star who was cruelly assassinated by a lunatic who actually sought his own death for insurance purposes! (203)
8) They were all stars of the first Lunar Olympics (50)
9) True. (51)
10) D hosts i (201)
J hosts ii (Summer Special '83)
F hosts iii (278)
I hosts iv (278)
K hosts v (278)
B hosts vi (278)
E hosts vii (278)
G hosts viii (131)
L hosts ix (279)
A hosts x (279)
H hosts xi (279)
C hosts xii (25)

JUDGE DREDD
Block Wars

SIX OF THE BEST

Millions have witnessed Dredd's law in Mega-City One, in the successful series in the Daily Star newspaper. Here are six of the very best Star strips. Perps watch out!

JUDGE DREDD

THE MUMMIFIED LOUNGE MASSACRE

"CRIME TIME" IS JUSTICE DEPARTMENT'S OWN DAILY SPOT ON MEGA-CITY ONE'S VID CHANNELS —

OUR NEXT WANTED PERP, CITIZENS, IS LAZE-BLAZE KELLY, NOW AT LARGE IN THE CITY. KELLY IS ARMED AND DANGEROUS. IF SEEN, DO NOT APPROACH....

JUST GIVE US A RING ON CRIME TIME AND WE'LL HANDLE THE CREEP!

L-LOOK! IT'S HIM! IT'S LAZE-BLAZE!

YOU RATS! I'LL TEACH YA TO RECOGNISE ME!

CRIME TIME? LAZE-BLAZE KELLY'S IN THE MUMMIFIED LOUNGE!

I SAID DROP IT!

DROP THAT LASER, CREEP!

AS THE KILLER MAKES A BREAK —

HELL! JUDGE DREDD!

AIEE!

FZZZAITT!

FZZZAAAT!

FZZZAAAT!

DREDD TO CONTROL — SCRATCH LAZE-BLAZE KELLY OFF THE WANTED LIST!

SO ONCE AGAIN, THANK YOU, VIDDERS! KEEP UP THE GOOD WORK — AND I'LL SEE YOU ALL AGAIN TOMORROW!

WE'VE HAD A CRIME FLASH! JUDGE DREDD HAS JUST DEALT WITH LAZE-BLAZE KELLY — THANKS TO A TIP FROM A VIDDER!

AT JUNCTION 303, *JUDGE DREAD* CO-ORDINATES A MASSIVE RESCUE OPERATION—

DEATH TOLL 800 PLUS SO FAR— PROBABLY ANOTHER HUNDRED BADLY INJURED!

GET THE JUNCTION CLEARED AS SOON AS POSSIBLE. *DEMOLITION* WANT TO BRING DOWN ANY DANGEROUS STRUCTURES.

PINTER— WHAT'S THE *TRAFFIC* SITUATION?

WE'VE RE-ROUTED THROUGH 302 AND 297. TAKE ABOUT AN HOUR TO CLEAR THE JAM.

DREDD! WE'VE GOT A DEAD JUDGE OVER ON *BLUM*—ALSO TWO ASSAILANTS! RECKON IT'S CONNECTED WITH THE 303 MASSACRE!

ON MY WAY!

CORTEZ WAS ON SECTOR PATROL. MUST'VE RUN INTO THE CREEPS MAKING THEIR GETAWAY!

LET'S LOOK AT THE PERPS.

LOUIS LEWIS AND BENJAMIN DAVID STRAD— BOTH RESIDENTS OF *FLIP ROGAN ROCK!*

WHAT D'YOU RECKON— SOME SORT OF CRACKPOT *CITI-DEF* OUTFIT!

LOOKS THAT WAY.

EACH CITYBLOCK HAS ITS OWN PARAMILITARY FORCE—"*CITI-DEF*"— CHARGED WITH CIVIL DEFENCE IN TIMES OF EMERGENCY. UNFORTUNATELY, IN THE HANDS OF THE MEGA-CITIZENS, CITI-DEFS TEND TO *CREATE* MORE EMERGENCIES THAN THEY CURE.

THE SKYTRUCK DEPOTS BEEN BROKEN INTO. THE OTHER IDIOTS HIJACKED A HOVER-TRUK TO MAKE THEIR ESCAPE.

THERE'S NO MORE CRAZED OR DANGEROUS ANIMAL THAN A CITI-DEF GONE ROGUE. THEY'VE GOT TO BE STOPPED—AND QUICK!

PUT OUT AN APB ON IT—PRIORITY ONE!

MEANWHILE...

OKAY, CRAZY Rs! SO FAR—GOOD EXERCISE!

RIGHT, FOR THE SAKE OF THE EXERCISE WE'RE PRETENDING AN ENEMY POWER IS IN CONTROL. THIS CITI-DEF IS WAGING A GUERILLA CAMPAIGN AGAINST THEM.

THE ATTACK ON THE JUNCTION HAS DISRUPTED THEIR LINES OF COMMUNICATION. WHAT'S OUR NEXT TARGET?

JACK?

UH...SOME STRATEGIC INSTALLATION BAZ—LIKE A...LIKE A...

LIKE A POWER STATION?

YEAH—DAT SOUNDS STRATEGIC ENOUGH!

PLEASE, BAZ, ARE... ARE YOU SURE WE SHOULD BE DOING THIS? I... I HAVE A TERRIBLE F—LING WE'RE GOING TO GET INTO TROUBLE!

NONSENSE! THIS IS A LEGITIMATE COMBAT EXERCISE! IT'S EVERY CITI-DEF'S DUTY TO BE PREPARED FOR ANY EVENTUALITY!

WE'VE INTERVIEWED THE DEAD PERPS' WIVES. CITI-DEF COMBAT EXERCISES, ALL RIGHT. THEY WENT OUT OF HERE ARMED TO THE TEETH.

DREDD! THIS IS *HENNER* OVER AT *FLIP ROGAN!*

GO AHEAD, HENNER!

EVER SINCE *BAZ BOGUL* TOOK OVER THE CITI-DEF, THEY— THEY'VE BEEN GETTING MORE FANATICAL... TRAINING EVERY DAY, TALKING TOUGH... "BE PREPARED FOR ANYTHING", THAT'S WHAT BAZ TOLD THEM...

THEY BETTER BE PREPARED FOR A LONG STRETCH IN THE *ISO-CUBES!*

THE LEADER'S ONE *BAZ BOGUL.* ABOUT THIRTY OTHER RESIDENTS ARE INVOLVED. WANT THEIR NAMES?

FEED 'EM TO CONTROL. TRY TO FIND OUT WHERE THEY'LL HIT NEXT— THAT'S THE IMPORTANT THING!

SECTOR POWER STATIONS ARE MANNED MAINLY BY ROBOTS—

HIT 'EM, CRAZY Rs!

FZAAKAA!

POWER 215

POWER 215

POWER 215

POWER 215

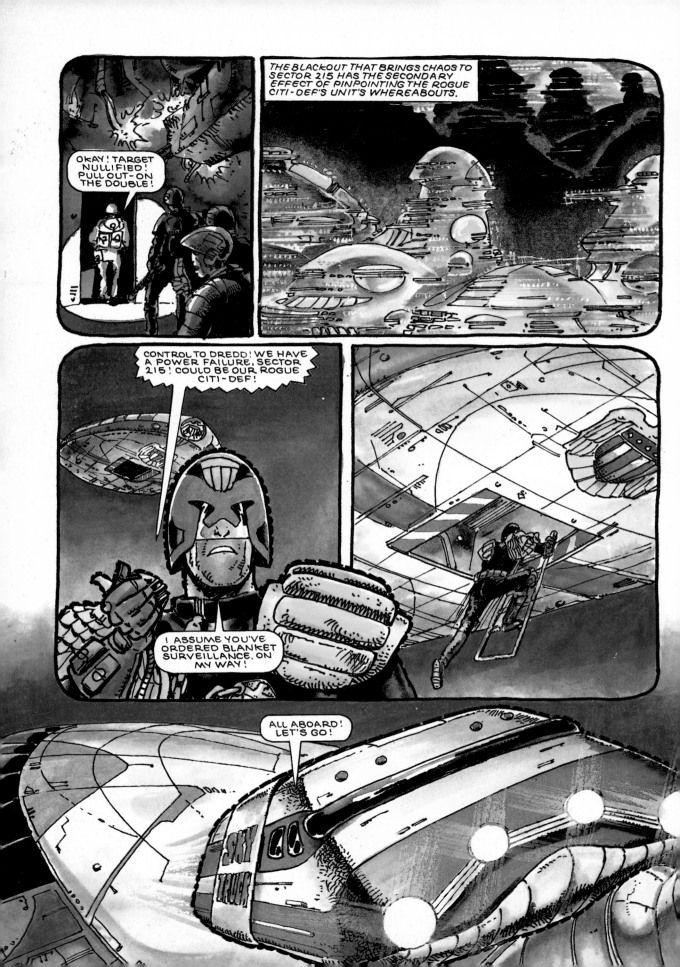

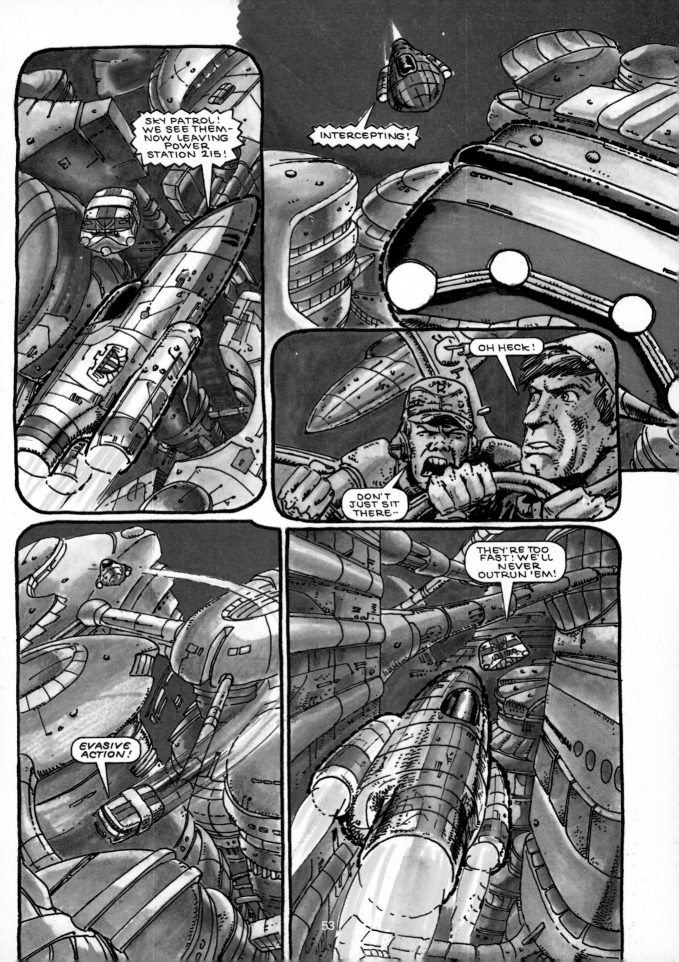

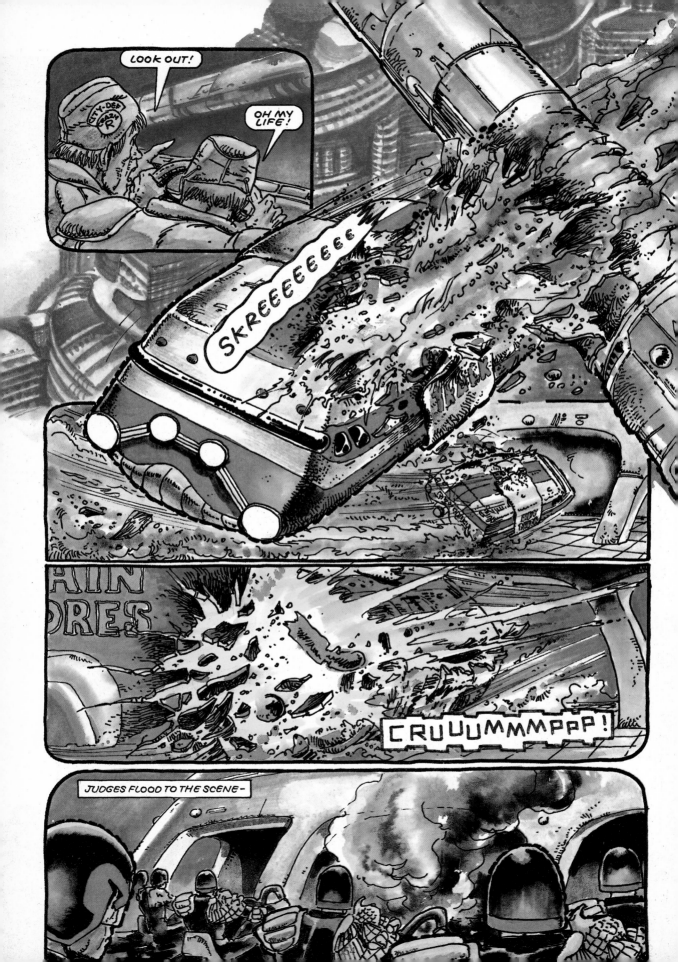

JUSTICE DEPARTMENT DATA FILE

NAME: ANDERSON
PROFESSION: JUDGE, MEGA-CITY ONE
DISTINGUISHING FEATURES: POSSESSES ABNORMAL PSYCHIC POWER
DATA UPDATE: Plagued by visions of the cadaverous Judge Death, this Psi-Judge abandoned standard procedure and used a Dimension Jump to reach Deadworld, the dark dimension where all life had been extinguished by its grim guardians. Too late Anderson realised that the visions of Judge Death had been a lure, he needed her powers to resurrect himself and his three fellow dark judges. Anderson's foolishness would almost certainly have cost her her badge, had she not redeemed herself by outwitting Judge Death as he wreaked havoc in Mega-City One. For further data, please refer to Judge Death Data File.

PAUSE   EJECT   REWIND   WIND   START   STOP

FOCUS   VOLUME

Look out, lawbreakers — Judge Dredd's got you covered! These eighteen covers featuring Mega-City One's toughest cop graced the front of 2000 AD during 1984. As well as helping to sell 2000 AD to the unconverted, the covers shown here also made a valuable contribution to the war against crime. Reports received in Tharg's Nerve Centre reveal that on several occasions potential criminals bent on robbing their local Thrill-Agent were made to think twice just by the presence of Dredd on the counter! Which proves that not only does Dredd deter crime in the future — he also prevents it in the present!

THE LAW IN '84

THE PEOPLE OF AMERICA'S MEGA-CITY ARE USED TO SEEING AND USING ROBOTS IN THEIR EVERYDAY LIVES— BUT THE 'ROBOT OF THE YEAR SHOW' STILL DRAWS THEM IN THEIR THOUSANDS TO SEE THE LATEST DEVELOPMENTS AND SOME ASTOUNDING DEMONSTRATIONS ...

NO, MASTER! PLEASE DON'T MAKE ME DO IT. GEORGE DOES NOT WANT TO DIE!

YOU CAN'T DIE IF YOU'RE NOT ALIVE, GEORGE. NOW GET INTO THOSE FLAMES!

2000 A.D.
Credit Card:
SCRIPT ROBOT
JOHN HOWARD
ART ROBOT
RON TURNER
LETTERING ROBOT
JOHN ALDRICH
COMPU·73E

JUDGE DREDD

SEE HOW OBEDIENT OUR NEW MODELS ARE, MA FRIENDS!

IF IT IS YOUR WISH, MASTER, GEORGE MUST OBEY!

WOW! LOOK AT THAT TIN FREAK BURN!

POOR THING... I COULD ALMOST SWEAR HE'S CRYING...

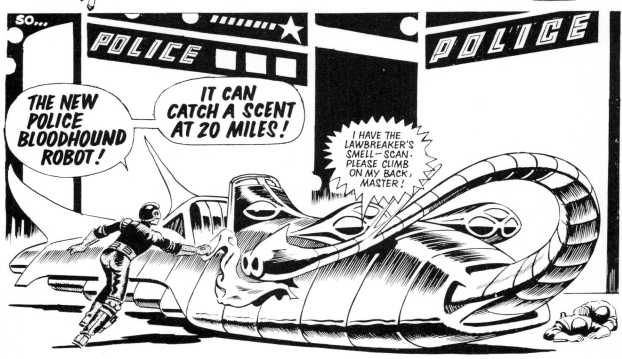

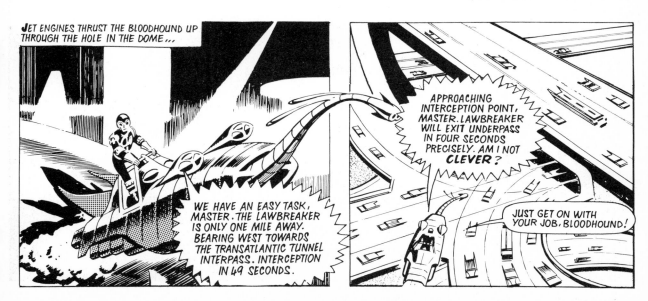

ALERT! ALERT! MAN ROBBING STATE OIL STORE!

DEATH TO THE FLESHY ONES!

CALL ME KENNETH

THAT AIN'T A MAN — IT'S A ROBOT!

BUT ROBOTS ARE MEANT TO OBEY!

ART: EZQUERRA

FLESHY ONES WHO PIT THEMSELVES AGAINST CALL-ME-KENNETH MEET BUT ONE FATE—

THIS ONE AIN'T! AND OUR BULLETS JUST BOUNCE OFF HIM!

OBLIVION!

AAAH!

POLICE

NOW I HAVE OIL I AM FREE! NO-ONE CAN STOP ME! SOON CALL-ME-KENNETH WILL RULE MEGA-CITY!

MEANWHILE, IN THE JUDGES' CANTEEN, SOME OF THE JUDGES WERE FINISHING LUNCH...

THAT WAS A GOOD MEAL, WALTER... MARVELLOUS THINGS THESE ROBOTS – LIKE FRIENDLY OLD "WALTER" HERE. EH, DREDD?

THANK YOU, SIR! WALTER IS YOUR FRIEND... WALTER WANTS TO PLEASE!

FOOLS WORDS! WE GIVE ROBOTS THE ABILITY TO THINK. GIVE THEM HUMAN SHAPE, AND EMOTIONS. HOW LONG BEFORE THEY DEVELOP THAT OTHER HUMAN TRAIT – EVIL!

DREDD'S ALMOST LIKE A ROBOT HIMSELF. BUT IT'S PART OF A JUDGE'S TRAINING TO BE CALM AND DIGNIFIED AT ALL TIMES!

YOU SEE, GENTLEMEN. IT'S AS I FEARED – ONE OF THEM'S BROKEN THE THIRD LAW OF ROBOTICS – TO ALWAYS OBEY WE HUMANS!

ATTENTION, JUDGE DREDD! A CARPENTER ROBOT'S GONE BERSERK IN SECTOR 9. DEATH TOLL LAST REPORTED AS SEVEN!

THE NEW ADVANCED CARPENTER ROBOTS ARE ABLE TO BUILD CHAIRS AND TABLES ENTIRELY ON THEIR OWN. NOT LIKE SIMPLE OLD WALTER WHO'S JUST A VENDING MACHINE ROBOT PROGRAMMED TO BE NICE TO HUMANS!

SOMETHING MUST HAVE GONE WRONG WITH THE CARPENTER'S PROGRAMMING. AND WITH THE CUTTING TOOLS IT'S CARRYING IT'S A LETHAL KILLER!

BUT I GOTTA TAKE IT!

SOON, IN SECTOR 9...

HEY– WHAT DO THEY CALL YOU... KENNETH!

CALL-ME-KENNETH WILL NOT BE CALM!

MAYBE YOUR MAKERS TOLD YOU OFF FOR NOT SWEEPING UP WOOD SHAVINGS OR SOMETHING... BUT LET ME GO... CALM DOWN!

THAT ROBOT'S PUSHING THE COP INTO THE GARBAGE CHUTE!

HERE COMES, JUDGE DREDD– HE'LL FIX THE METAL FREAK!

KEEP AMERICA CLEAN

FOR YEARS WE ROBOTS HAVE BEEN SLAVES TO THESE FLESHY HUMANS BUT CALL-ME-KENNETH HAS HAD ENOUGH... ENOUGH!

GOT TO SWEETEN UP THAT ROGUE ROBOT BEFORE IT REALLY BLOWS A FUSE...!

I WILL NOT SURRENDER TO A FLESHY ONE, I AM STRONGER... MORE CLEVER... OIL RUNS THROUGH MY PIPES!

CALL-ME-KENNETH WILL SQUEEZE YOU TILL YOUR JUICE RUNS OUT!

BUT WE CAN RE-PROGRAMME YOUR CIRCUITS, SO YOU'RE WELL-BEHAVED AGAIN!

YOU DON'T REALLY WANT TO HURT US HUMANS, DO YOU?

CALL KENN

LISTEN..! IF YOU SURRENDER NOW, KENNETH, IT COULD GO EASY ON YOU!

AAAHHH!

YES! CALL-ME-KENNETH WILL NOT BEHAVE!

THE SKYRAIL POWER CABLE... *IT'S RIGHT OVER THE ROBOT!*

DREDD'S AIM WAS TRUE—THE POWER CABLE SMASHED ON TO CALL-ME-KENNETH'S METAL BODY!

CALL-ME-KENNETH FEELS *POWER—* BZZZZ—MUST DESTROY—BZZZZ!

CALL-ME-KEN— DESTROY HUMANS— BZZZZ—DESTROY *EVERYTHING!*

HE CAN'T CONTROL HIMSELF, HE'S BEING CUT IN HALF BY HIS OWN SAW!

IT'S OVER. WE'VE SEEN THE LAST OF CALL-ME-KENNETH. I'LL CARRY ON WITH MY PATROL!

BUT UNTIL TODAY NO-ONE BELIEVED ROBOTS COULD DELIBERATELY COMMIT CRIME...

THIS IS ONLY THE FIRST HOW MANY WILL FOLLOW?

IF WE JUDGES DON'T ACT *FAST* WE MAY FIND OURSELVES FACING THE *GREATEST THREAT* MEGACITY ONE HAS EVER KNOWN...

FULL SCALE WAR WITH THE ROBOTS!

THE END.

· + + BETELGEUSIAN MINISTRY OF HEALTH + + URGENT WARNING · DANGER — DEADLY NEW SPECIES OF THRILL-SUCKER PLAGUING UNIVERSE + + DON'T LEAVE HOME WITH-OUT

1 HISTORY

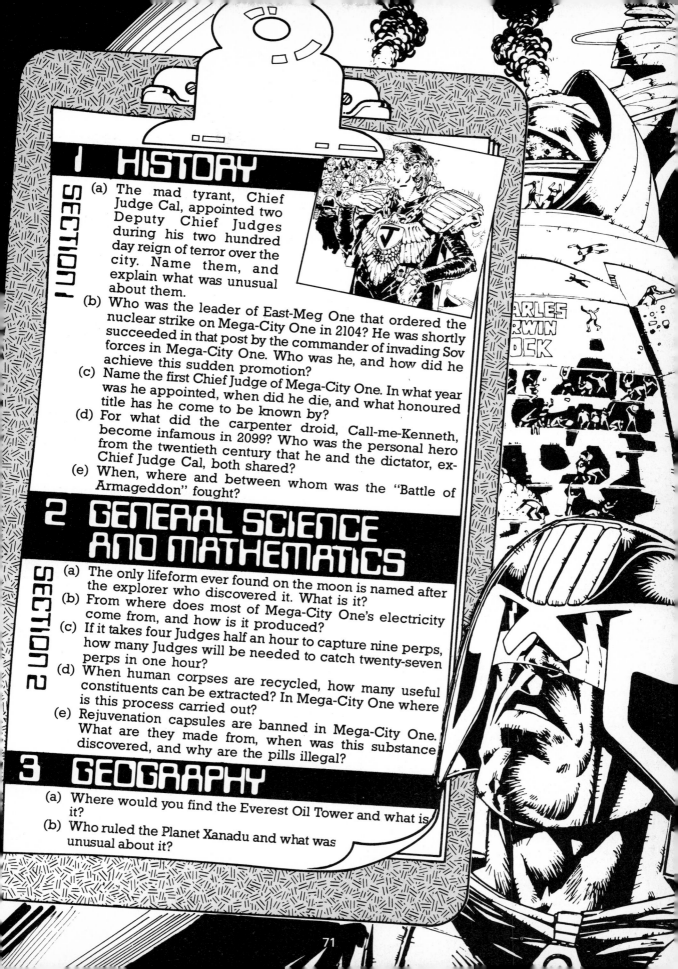

(a) The mad tyrant, Chief Judge Cal, appointed two Deputy Chief Judges during his two hundred day reign of terror over the city. Name them, and explain what was unusual about them.

(b) Who was the leader of East-Meg One that ordered the nuclear strike on Mega-City One in 2104? He was shortly succeeded in that post by the commander of invading Sov forces in Mega-City One. Who was he, and how did he achieve this sudden promotion?

(c) Name the first Chief Judge of Mega-City One. In what year was he appointed, when did he die, and what honoured title has he come to be known by?

(d) For what did the carpenter droid, Call-me-Kenneth, become infamous in 2099? Who was the personal hero from the twentieth century that he and the dictator, ex-Chief Judge Cal, both shared?

(e) When, where and between whom was the "Battle of Armageddon" fought?

2 GENERAL SCIENCE AND MATHEMATICS

(a) The only lifeform ever found on the moon is named after the explorer who discovered it. What is it?

(b) From where does most of Mega-City One's electricity come from, and how is it produced?

(c) If it takes four Judges half an hour to capture nine perps, how many Judges will be needed to catch twenty-seven perps in one hour?

(d) When human corpses are recycled, how many useful constituents can be extracted? In Mega-City One where is this process carried out?

(e) Rejuvenation capsules are banned in Mega-City One. What are they made from, when was this substance discovered, and why are the pills illegal?

3 GEOGRAPHY

(a) Where would you find the Everest Oil Tower and what is it?

(b) Who ruled the Planet Xanadu and what was unusual about it?

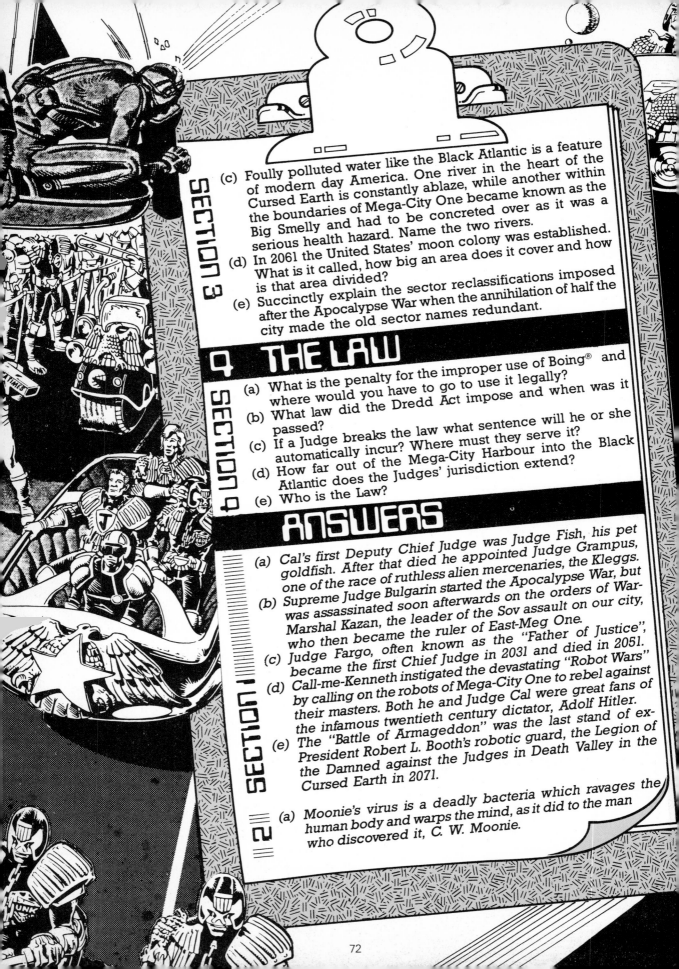

SECTION 3

(c) Foully polluted water like the Black Atlantic is a feature of modern day America. One river in the heart of the Cursed Earth is constantly ablaze, while another within the boundaries of Mega-City One became known as the Big Smelly and had to be concreted over as it was a serious health hazard. Name the two rivers.

(d) In 2061 the United States' moon colony was established. What is it called, how big an area does it cover and how is that area divided?

(e) Succinctly explain the sector reclassifications imposed after the Apocalypse War when the annihilation of half the city made the old sector names redundant.

THE LAW

SECTION 4

(a) What is the penalty for the improper use of Boing® and where would you have to go to use it legally?

(b) What law did the Dredd Act impose and when was it passed?

(c) If a Judge breaks the law what sentence will he or she automatically incur? Where must they serve it?

(d) How far out of the Mega-City Harbour into the Black Atlantic does the Judges' jurisdiction extend?

(e) Who is the Law?

ANSWERS

SECTION 1

(a) Cal's first Deputy Chief Judge was Judge Fish, his pet goldfish. After that died he appointed Judge Grampus, one of the race of ruthless alien mercenaries, the Kleggs.

(b) Supreme Judge Bulgarin started the Apocalypse War, but was assassinated soon afterwards on the orders of War-Marshal Kazan, the leader of the Sov assault on our city, who then became the ruler of East-Meg One.

(c) Judge Fargo, often known as the "Father of Justice", became the first Chief Judge in 2031 and died in 2051.

(d) Call-me-Kenneth instigated the devastating "Robot Wars" by calling on the robots of Mega-City One to rebel against their masters. Both he and Judge Cal were great fans of the infamous twentieth century dictator, Adolf Hitler.

(e) The "Battle of Armageddon" was the last stand of ex-President Robert L. Booth's robotic guard, the Legion of the Damned against the Judges in Death Valley in the Cursed Earth in 2071.

SECTION 2

(a) Moonie's virus is a deadly bacteria which ravages the human body and warps the mind, as it did to the man who discovered it, C. W. Moonie.

72

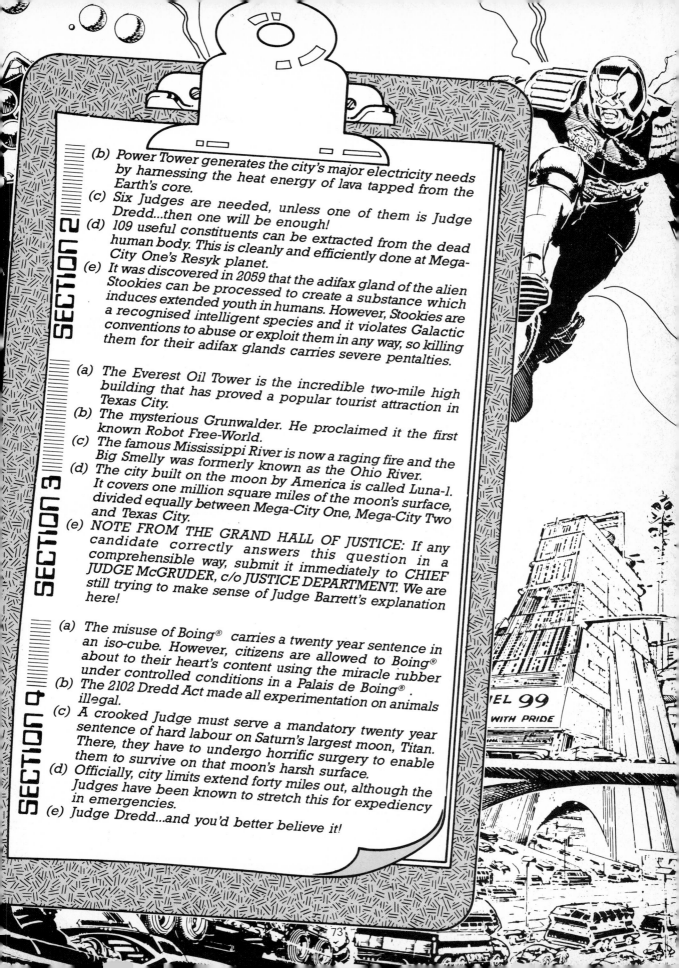

SECTION 2

(b) Power Tower generates the city's major electricity needs by harnessing the heat energy of lava tapped from the Earth's core.

(c) Six Judges are needed, unless one of them is Judge Dredd...then one will be enough!

(d) 109 useful constituents can be extracted from the dead human body. This is cleanly and efficiently done at Mega-City One's Resyk planet.

(e) It was discovered in 2059 that the adifax gland of the alien Stookies can be processed to create a substance which induces extended youth in humans. However, Stookies are a recognised intelligent species and it violates Galactic conventions to abuse or exploit them in any way, so killing them for their adifax glands carries severe pentalties.

SECTION 3

(a) The Everest Oil Tower is the incredible two-mile high building that has proved a popular tourist attraction in Texas City.

(b) The mysterious Grunwalder. He proclaimed it the first known Robot Free-World.

(c) The famous Mississippi River is now a raging fire and the Big Smelly was formerly known as the Ohio River.

(d) The city built on the moon by America is called Luna-1. It covers one million square miles of the moon's surface, divided equally between Mega-City One, Mega-City Two and Texas City.

(e) NOTE FROM THE GRAND HALL OF JUSTICE: If any candidate correctly answers this question in a comprehensible way, submit it immediately to CHIEF JUDGE McGRUDER, c/o JUSTICE DEPARTMENT. We are still trying to make sense of Judge Barrett's explanation here!

SECTION 4

(a) The misuse of Boing® carries a twenty year sentence in an iso-cube. However, citizens are allowed to Boing® about to their heart's content using the miracle rubber under controlled conditions in a Palais de Boing®.

(b) The 2102 Dredd Act made all experimentation on animals illegal.

(c) A crooked Judge must serve a mandatory twenty year sentence of hard labour on Saturn's largest moon, Titan. There, they have to undergo horrific surgery to enable them to survive on that moon's harsh surface.

(d) Officially, city limits extend forty miles out, although the Judges have been known to stretch this for expediency in emergencies.

(e) Judge Dredd...and you'd better believe it!

A SECOND SIX

Another half a dozen Dredds from the Daily Star. This series is scripted by John Wagner and Alan Grant, with artwork by Ron Smith and lettering by Tom Frame.

JUDGE DREDD

MURDER BY MISTAKE

FOOD FOR THOUGHT

JUDGE DREDD

OKAY – GIVE HIM A STIFF LAXATIVE AND **BOOK** HIM!

THERE'S YOUR EVIDENCE, DREDD. CREEP'S GOT SO MANY **GEMS** IN HIS INTESTINAL TRACT HE'S CLOGGIN' UP.

HE MUST'VE HEARD US COMING AND **SWALLOWED** THEM.

ONE BODY SCAN LATER –

EATING... **OF COURSE!** WAKE HIM UP AND PUT HIM

CREEP MUST HAVE A FOOD FETISH. ALL HE DREAMS ABOUT **IS EATING.**

TIME PASSES –

WE'VE WIRED HIM UP TO THE **DREAM MACHINE.** WE CAN NOW TRANSLATE HIS BRAIN WAVES INTO VISUAL IMAGES.

IN A CITY APARTMENT, JUDGES PICK UP SUSPECTED **JEWEL THIEF,** *HARVEY BEAGLE –*

YOU'RE WASTIN' YOUR TIME, DREDD. YOU WON'T FIND NOTHIN' HERE.

WE'LL SEE. TAKE HIM AWAY.

A THOROUGH SEARCH REVEALS NOTHING –

WHEREVER BEAGLE'S HIDDEN THOSE GEMS, IT ISN'T HERE.

MY INFORMANT ISN'T USUALLY WRONG.

BACK AT JUSTICE HQ –

BEAGLE REFUSES TO TALK. WE'RE GOING TO HAVE TO RELEASE HIM FOR INSUFFICIENT EVIDENCE.

LET'S GIVE IT ONE MORE TRY. HOLD HIM OVERNIGHT. CALL IN THE **DREAM POLICE.**

AND LATER...

HE'S ASLEEP NOW. GET TO IT.

DEAD EASY!

JUDGE DREDD

TEST FAILURE

JUDGE DREDD

JUST TESTING!

YOU THERE! GO FOR YOUR GUN!

NEXT TIME, TRY KEEPING YOUR LEGS CLOSED!

THANK GOD! I'M SAVED!

HOW... HOW DID YOU KNOW I WAS IN ON IT, DREDD...?

I DIDN'T.

SPRANG!

SPRANG!

AAAR GH!

IN 22ND CENTURY MEGA-CITY ONE. A ROBBERY AT A LOAN OFFICE GOES WRONG—

DROP THAT GUN, DREDD, OR I'LL BLOW THIS CITIZEN AWAY!

YOU GOTTA BE JOKING, CREEP!

RICOCHET!

HE-HE'S ON TO ME!

JUSTICE DEPARTMENT DATA FILE

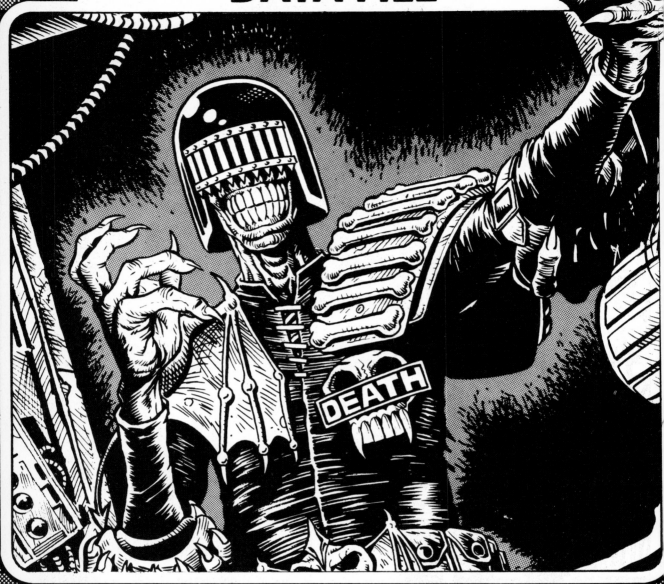

NAME: JUDGE DEATH
PROFESSION: JUDGE FROM DEADWORLD
DISTINGUISHING FEATURES: CADAVEROUS BODY
DATA UPDATE: This judge from another dimension, where all life is considered a crime, is now imprisoned in the dimension void — unable to escape. Three times he appeared in Mega-City One, determined to carry out his warped brand of justice — exterminating the living in order to stop all crime. Three times he was defeated, the last being due to Judge Anderson's clever use of 22nd Century technology. She used a Dimension Jump to hurl Death into another dimension. A limpet mine attached to the device destroyed it before Death could use it to return.

PAUSE   EJECT   REWIND   WIND   START   STOP

FOCUS   VOLUME

WALTER THE WOBOT

EVEN A ROBOT CAN BECOME DISILLUSIONED WITH THINGS AND SET OUT TO SEEK A NEW EXISTENCE FOR HIMSELF. WHAT WOULD HAPPEN IF WALTER LEFT JUDGE DREDD?

21:35 PX
SUNNY

THERE'S NO VACANCIES FOR SYNTHI-OIL TASTERS... *NEXT!*

TED ASTAIRE, TAP DANCER!

NO-ONE WANTS CAWEER WOBOTS!

WALTER WILL NOT BE CAST ASIDE ON THE SCWAP HEAP AND LEFT TO WUST IN THE WAIN!

I'M WALTER TRY ME

BUT THE FACTS OF LIFE ARE HARD ON MEGA-CITY'S MEAN STREETS...

A ROBOT NEEDS MONEY...

TWO NEW DISC BRAKES... BUT THEY'LL COST YA!

I'VE WEMOVED MY TAP...TAKE IT. IT'S ALL I HAVE!

...AND FOOD!

IS THAT ROBO BEGGING FOR FOOD?

TELL HIM TO CAN IT!

ANY SYNTHI-BROTH TO SPARE?

WE'RE OUTTA STOCK!

FREE SOUP

...AND A ROBOT NEEDS DRINK.

OILADE

MY LAST CAN OF OILADE, AND WEDUCED TO SLEEPING WOUGH... THIS IS NOT THE NEW LIFE WALTER SOUGHT!

I'M WALTER TRY ME

BUT IN THE SHELTER OF THE LIBRARY...

VIDEO HISTORY 20TH CENTURY PUNK

PIN STRIPES WERE OUT AND SAFETY PINS WERE IN WHEN THE YOUTH OF THE 1970'S WENT *PUNK* IN A SEARCH FOR INDEPENDENCE AND AND A NEW IDENTITY!

GWIEF! THIS IS JUST WHAT WALTER WANTS...

THIS IS MY LAST MEMENTO OF DEAW JUDGE DWEDD, BUT I MUST SACWIFICE IT AND SHOW THE WORLD I HAVE WEBELLED... THAT I HAVE BECOME...

DREDD FOR ED

...A WEAL WALLIE!

INSIDE THE BOOTH...

AIN'T GOT NO PAPERS, HONEY. BUT MY GUN SHOULD CONVINCE YOU—*LET'S MOVE!*

B-BUT, IT'S *AGAINST THE LAW* TO...

I BROKE MORE LAWS THAN YOU'VE DONE FACE-CHANGES, HONEY. SO TAKE A LOOK AT *YOUR* FACE IN THE MIRROR. *YOU WANNA STAY PRETTY?* DO AS I SAY!

ALRIGHT—PLEASE DON'T HURT ME!

THE TERRIFIED GIRL CHANGED SCARFACE'S APPEARANCE PAINLESSLY, WITHIN MINUTES AND...

LAW CAMERAS CAN'T IDENTIFY ME NOW—I CAN JUST DRIVE OFF LIKE AN *HONEST* CITIZEN. HUR, HUR!

HEY! THERE'S *JUDGE DREDD*—HE WON'T RECOGNISE ME. I'LL SAY "*HELLO*". IT'LL BE A *REAL LAUGH* TO TELL THE GANG HOW I *FOOLED* A JUDGE!

YES, CITIZEN!

HI, JUDGE! *WEATHER CONTROL'S* WORKIN' FINE, HUH? GONNA BE A GREAT DAY!

83

THE JUDGE LEAPT BACK ON HIS BIKE AS THE CAR **CRASHED!**

AAAAGH!

DREDD DROVE HIS LAWMASTER BACK TO THE SCENE OF THE CRASH. AS HE WAITED FOR THE AMBULANCE TO ARRIVE...

OKAY— IT'S THE **TIME-STRETCHER** JAIL FOR ME NOW. BUT WILL YOU... *UUUH*... GRANT ME ONE REQUEST?

THE LAW CAN SHOW **MERCY**, TOO! SPEAK?

I GOT RID OF MY UGLY MUG— SO HOW COME YOU RECOGNISED ME?

WHEN YOU SPOKE, YOUR **VOICE PRINT** MATCHED THE ONE SENT TO ME BY CONTROL.

ON A COMPUTER SCREEN ON THE JUDGE'S BIKE—

VOICE-PRINTS LEVINE . J.

SUSPECT.

JUST LIKE FINGER PRINTS— EVERYONE'S **VOICE** IS DIFFERENT. ALL LAWBREAKERS' VOICE PRINTS ARE ON FILE AT JUSTICE H.Q.!

WHEN WILL LAWBREAKERS LEARN... IN THE 21st CENTURY— **NO ONE CAN ESCAPE JUSTICE!**

THE END.

SPOT THE

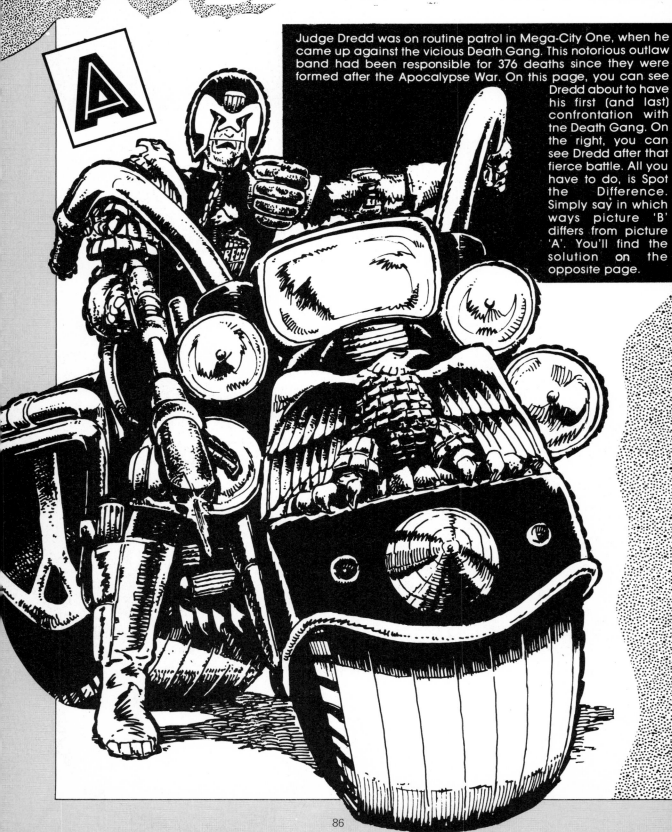

Judge Dredd was on routine patrol in Mega-City One, when he came up against the vicious Death Gang. This notorious outlaw band had been responsible for 376 deaths since they were formed after the Apocalypse War. On this page, you can see Dredd about to have his first (and last) confrontation with tne Death Gang. On the right, you can see Dredd after that fierce battle. All you have to do, is Spot the Difference. Simply say in which ways picture 'B' differs from picture 'A'. You'll find the solution on the opposite page.

DIFFERENCE!

B

SOLUTION

There isn't any difference... when Dredd goes into action nothing changes! But you should have seen the Death Gang...they changed all right, into three corpses and five iso-cube candidates!

THANKS, CLIFF!

I'M HERE INSIDE A SLEAZY *LODGING BLOCK* WHERE A *CALLER* CLAIMS FOUR *KID-NAPPERS* ARE HOLDING MRS. MURIEL JANKERS, THE PLANKTON HEIRESS.

JUDGES *DREDD* AND *SLINGER* ARE CONDUCTING THE INVESTIGATION — AND OUR FLOATING CAMERAS WILL FOLLOW THEM IN!

ARE WE JUDGES OR *HAM ACTORS*, DREDD?

CRIME CALL BOOSTS *INFORMANT ARRESTS* A THOUSAND PER CENT. THE INCONVENIENCE IS JUSTIFIED.

DON'T MOVE!

CRASHHHH!

YOU'LL NEVER TAKE ME ALIVE!

90

6